EYEWITNESS ◉ JUNIORS

AMAZING BIRDS

WRITTEN BY

ALEXANDRA PARSONS

PHOTOGRAPHED BY

JERRY YOUNG

DK

DORLING KINDERSLEY

London • New York • Moscow • Sydney

DK

A DORLING KINDERSLEY BOOK

Editor Scott Steadman
Designers Ann Cannings and Margo Beamish-White
Senior art editor Jacquie Gulliver
Editorial director Sue Unstead
Art director Anne-Marie Bulat

Special photography by Jerry Young
Illustrations by Mark Iley and John Bendall
Animals supplied by Trevor Smith's Animal World
Editorial consultants The staff of the Natural History Museum, London

Published in Great Britain by
Dorling Kindersley Limited
9 Henrietta Street, London WC2E 8PS

Paperback edition
2 4 6 8 10 9 7 5 3 1

Copyright © 1990, 1998 Dorling Kindersley Limited, London

Visit us on the World Wide Web at
http://www.dk.com

A CIP catalogue record for this book is available from the British Library.

ISBN 0-7513-5762-6

Colour reproduction by Colourscan, Singapore
Printed and bound in Singapore by Imago

Contents

What is a bird?

There are 9,000 different kinds of bird – birds that sing and birds that squawk, pretty birds and plain ones, huge birds and tiny ones, birds that soar high in the sky and birds that cannot fly at all.

Flap flop
Humans have always wanted to fly like the birds. The first people to build flying machines copied bird wings and tried to flap with their arms. But the human body is just not made for flying.

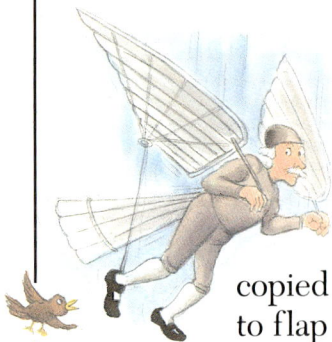

Looking back
Most birds have good eyesight, and owls see especially well. They can swivel their heads almost right around to see in every direction.

The silent hunter
Owls hunt at night, when most other birds are asleep. They take small animals like mice by surprise because they can fly so quietly.

What have they got?
All birds have two legs, two wings, a beak, and hundreds of feathers. And they all lay eggs.

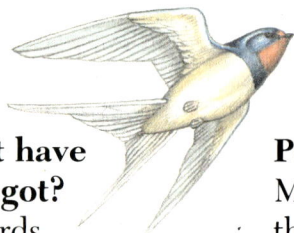

Pointy toes
Most birds have four toes. Birds that perch on small branches have three toes pointing forward, while birds that climb trees have two pointing forward and two pointing back. Water birds have webs between their toes.

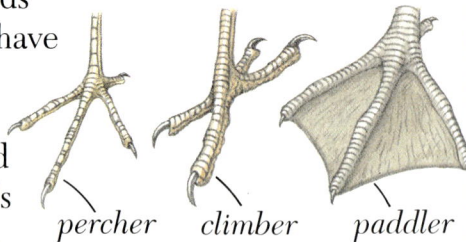

percher   *climber*   *paddler*

An owl's "ears" are really just tufts of feathers.

Eagle owl

This rare bird is the largest owl of all. It may not look very fierce, but it can kill and eat a small fox.

Feathers

Birds have three kinds of feathers. Flight feathers in their wings and tails help them to fly, and downy feathers keep them warm. Body feathers cover the rest of their bodies.

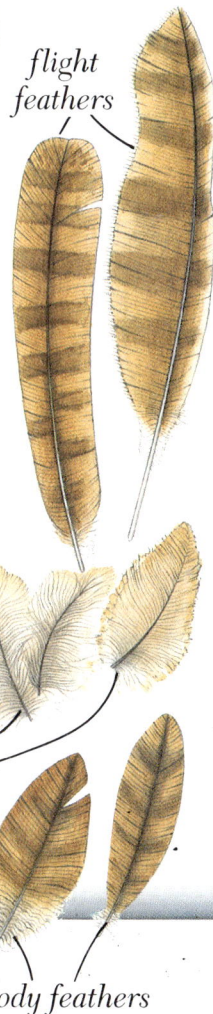

flight feathers

Barn owl

This little owl roosts and makes its nest in barns and old buildings. It couldn't tackle anything much larger than a field mouse.

downy feathers

The eagle owl has huge claws, or "talons".

body feathers

The flamingo

This remarkable bird has very long legs, a very long neck, and a beak that works like a huge sieve. It lives around salty lakes and rivers in the warm parts of the world, from Africa to the Caribbean.

Sift and sieve
The flamingo's beak has little sieves on either side. To eat, the bird slurps in a beakful of water, then uses its tongue to push it all out again through the sieves. Only the tiniest, juiciest titbits are left behind.

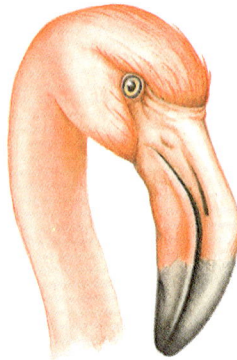

Daily milk
Just like a human baby, a flamingo chick lives on a kind of milk. Both parents dribble a bright red liquid from their beaks when the hungry baby starts to squawk.

Togetherness
Flamingos like to stick together. Sometimes they live in flocks of over a million birds.

Mud pies
A flamingo nest is not much to look at. The male and female build it together, using their beaks to push blobs of mud into a big pile.

Heads down
To eat, flamingos poke their heads into the water upside-down. Some feed on tiny plants, called algae, which float in the water. Others prefer trawling the mud for shrimps.

Why is the flamingo pink?

Because of the food it eats. Pink colouring in algae and shrimps passes into the bird's body and comes out in its feathers.

Party treat

A long time ago, in Ancient Rome, pickled flamingo tongues were considered a very special treat. At feasts they were served up on golden dishes.

To make feeding easier, a flamingo's knees bend backwards – unlike yours.

Some flamingos are pinker than others, but they all have a few black feathers in their wings.

The lesser flamingo

There are six different kinds of flamingo. This one is called the lesser flamingo and it comes from Africa.

Parrots

There are more than 300 kinds of parrot, and most of them are very colourful. Many live in tropical forests, high up among the trees. Others live in open bush country.

Fluffy face
Many parrots fluff up the feathers on their heads when they are excited or angry.

When a bird flaps its wings, it's the long feathers at the tips that lift it in the air.

Singsong
Most parrots do not have songs of their own – just very loud squawks. But some of them will sing any song that you teach them.

The kakapo
This rare New Zealand parrot cannot fly. Instead, it hops around the forest floor at night.

Jet set
The little Alexandrine parakeet, a kind of parrot, is found in the jungles of Asia. It whizzes through the trees very, very fast indeed.

Pretty parrot

This parrot is called the green-winged macaw. It comes from South America. Macaws are popular pets because they can be taught to copy human voices – and they like a lot of attention. They may live for over 30 years.

Heave-ho

Some parrots' beaks are so strong they can use them to haul themselves up trees.

nut eater   *insect eater*

Beaks to order

Birds' beaks help them catch their favourite food. Nuts and seeds crack in a parrot's short, strong beak. Insects are snapped up in a long, thin bill. Slippery fish are gripped firmly in a saw-edged beak.

fish eater

Hold on tight

Birds have to sleep without falling off their perches. They have a long, string-like tendon attached to each toe. While they sleep, this tendon locks the toes around the branch.

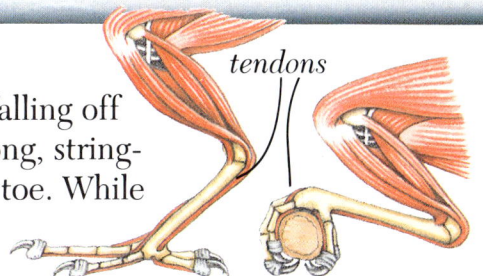

tendons

The pelican

This unusual bird looks clumsy waddling on land with its big body, stubby legs, and webbed feet. It is a water bird, born to fly and glide, or swim and catch fish in its built-in fishing net.

Swoop and scoop
The pelican's amazing beak has a very stretchy pouch. A brown pelican can plunge into the water and scoop up fish in its beak like a fisherman with a net.

Leaky beak
The pelican scoops up a lot of water as it fishes. It has to spill the water out of its beak before taking off – otherwise it would be too heavy to fly!

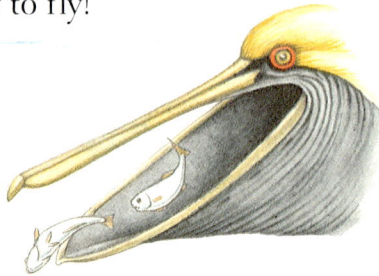

Bare babies
Baby pelicans hatch from their eggs without any feathers at all. But within three days they are covered in soft, brown down.

A lot of lunch

Grown-up pelicans eat an awful lot. They can gobble up as much as 5 kg of fish a day – that's the same as 20 school lunches!

Water birds have a coating of special oil on their feathers, so that the water slides right off them.

Holiday time

In the autumn, many birds fly somewhere warm where there is lots to eat. This Dalmatian pelican leaves Yugoslavia to spend the winter sunning itself by the Nile in Egypt.

Open wide!

When the mother pelican has a beak full of fish, she flies back to the nest to feed her chicks. The little pelicans stick their heads right into her pouch and eat their fill.

The vulture

Vultures are nature's rubbish collectors. They feed on dead bodies, eating everything except the bones.

Sunbathing

Like all birds, vultures have oils in their feathers to keep them clean. After a meal, the birds sit with their wings out to soak up the sunlight, which keeps their oils in shape.

Feeling peckish?

This is a hooded vulture from Africa. It's a big bird that sits up in trees looking and waiting for some poor creature to die.

Vultures have very powerful, curved beaks for ripping flesh off bones.

Rare bird
The California condor is part of the vulture family. It is one of the biggest, rarest – and ugliest – birds in the world.

In for the kill
Vultures gather quickly around a dying animal. As soon as one bird goes for the corpse, the whole flock will come rushing down. They can pick an antelope's bones clean in 20 minutes.

Blush pink
This fierce-looking bird actually blushes! At least, that's what it looks like. When a vulture is angry or excited, the bare skin around its face turns pink.

Cancel the concert
You won't get much of a song from a vulture. They just hiss and grunt in a nasty way.

The penguin

These smartly dressed black-and-white birds live among the icebergs in the cold Antarctic Ocean. Penguins are water birds that cannot fly. But they can swim very well, using their wings as flippers to "fly" through the water.

Thanks, Dad!
Keeping an egg warm on the ice is a difficult business. The father emperor penguin balances the egg on his feet, tucked under a cosy flap of skin.

Well caught!
Penguins catch all their food underwater. They can move really fast, and their spiky tongues help them to grip slippery fish in their beaks.

Welcome home, dear!
After the mother emperor penguin has laid the egg, she waddles off to sea for a good feed. Father penguin has to shuffle around for two whole months with his baby on his feet, unable to get to the sea and catch fish. He is very pleased to see the mother penguin when she finally comes back.

Tobogganing
The best way to get about on snow and ice is to slide. That's what penguins do, using their fat bellies as toboggans.

Nursery school
When baby penguins have grown large enough, they often gather together for safety while their parents go fishing.

The penguin has a thick blanket of fat under its skin for warmth.

Flat feet
The penguin uses its big webbed feet like the rudder of a boat, to steer itself in the water.

Waterproof suit
A penguin's body is covered with three layers of tiny, waterproof feathers, to keep it warm and dry in and out of the water.

Good swimmer
A penguin is an odd shape for a bird – it looks more like a seal. Its sleek body is perfect for diving and swimming. This fine fellow is a Humboldt penguin.

The swan

The graceful swan is one of the largest water birds. It glides along lakes and slow-moving rivers, feeding on grass and water weeds.

A swan has 25,000 feathers – more than any other bird.

Fairy tale swans

There is a Danish fairy tale about a whole family of princes who are turned into swans. They have to fly off and fetch their sister to help break the spell.

Built-in paddles

Swans have big webbed feet to help them paddle along in the water and waddle about on the shore.

A warm nest

Once a year the mute swan builds a huge nest out of grass and reeds. In it the female lays 5 to 8 eggs, each as big as your fist.

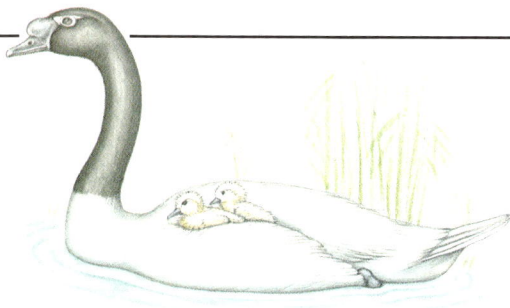

Hitching a ride

Young swans are called cygnets (*sig-nits*). They often ride around on their mother's back.

Black magic

Black swans come from Australia. Like all swans, they are very faithful birds. The male and female will stay together for years, looking after their little ones and teaching them to fly and swim.

A honk or a whistle?

This swan is called a mute swan and it honks. Most swans whistle.

Ugly duckling

Cygnets are a dull grey colour and a bit clumsy. Their feathers don't turn elegantly white until they are about three years old.

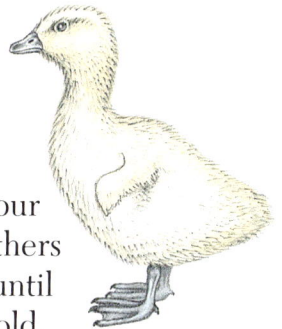

The peacock

The male peacock has a fabulous fan. He uses it to woo the dull-looking female, or peahen.

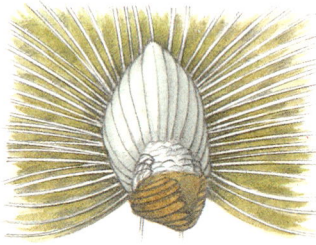

Rear view
The peacock's fan is not a tail. It's made of back feathers and is called a train. The bird's real tail holds the train up.

Backwards shuffle
The peacock only opens his fan when he's trying to charm a peahen. First he backs up to her. Then he spins suddenly to face her and dazzle her with his beautiful, quivering train.

Alarm call
Both the peacock and the peahen have good eyesight and hearing, so they are quick to sense danger. When they feel threatened, they give an incredibly loud shriek. This noise often warns other birds and animals in the forest.

Hypnotic eyes

The shimmering "eyes" on the peacock's train are a beautiful sight. They certainly fascinate the peahen – she may even be hypnotized by them.

Tail of love

The male lyrebird of Australia has a tail for charming females too. It looks just like a "lyre", a harp played in Greece long ago.

Look at me!

"As vain as a peacock" – that's what we call anyone who struts around in fancy clothes with their nose in the air.

A peacock's train can be 2 m high – taller than an average man.

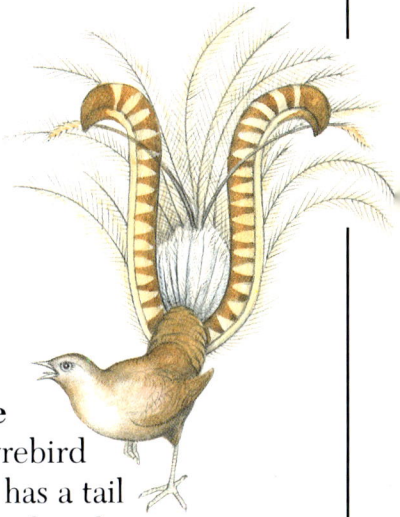

On the run

You might think a peacock would trip over his great long train, but he doesn't. With the feathers trailing behind him, he can run through the forest quickly and quietly.

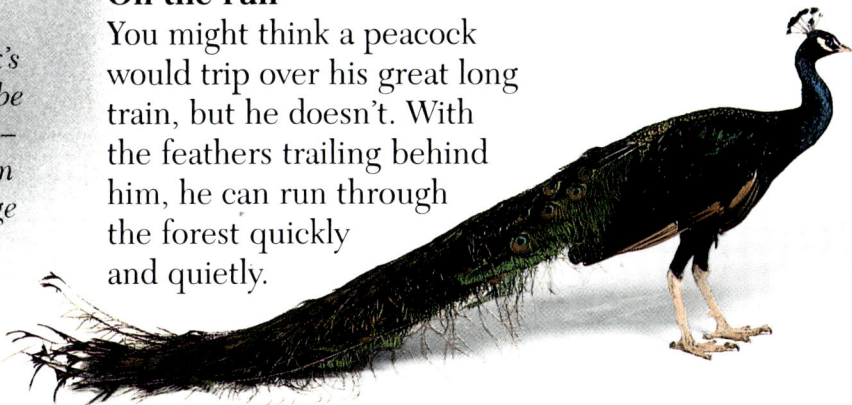

The ostrich

The biggest birds in the world can't fly at all. But they can certainly run. The African ostrich can zip along at up to 70 km/h, which is faster than the fastest sprinter.

A real rhea
This is a type of ostrich called a rhea (*ree-ah*). It lives in South America.

Shoulder high
A tall man standing next to an ostrich only comes up to the bird's shoulders.

What a dish!
Imagine eating an ostrich egg! One egg is bigger than a grapefruit and as heavy as 4,500 hummingbird eggs.

South American feather duster

Like all ostriches, the rhea has beautiful, soft feathers. In South America they are used to make feather dusters.

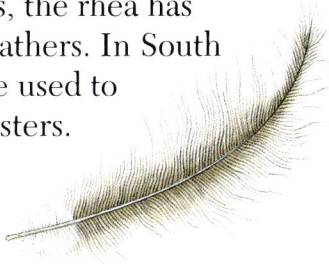

On the move

Ostriches roam the grassy plains of Africa in groups. They often join herds of antelope or cattle.

Bugs and greens

The rhea lives on leaves, grass, and insects. The bird spots food easily with its huge eyes and snaps it up in its big, flat beak.

Fashionable bird

Ostrich feathers are much admired and were once used to decorate hats and dresses. The cream-coloured shells of ostrich eggs were even made into table decorations.

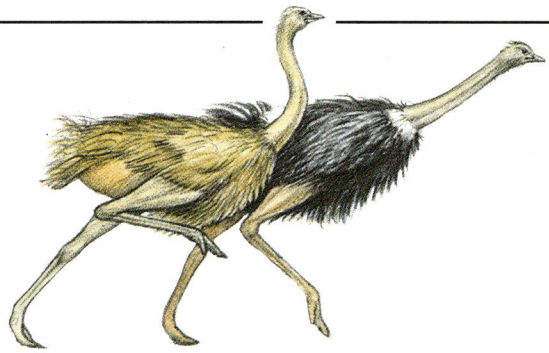

Walking on cushions

The African ostrich is the only bird that has just two toes. Each toe has a soft pad like a cushion underneath it, to stop the heavy ostrich from sinking into the soft sand.

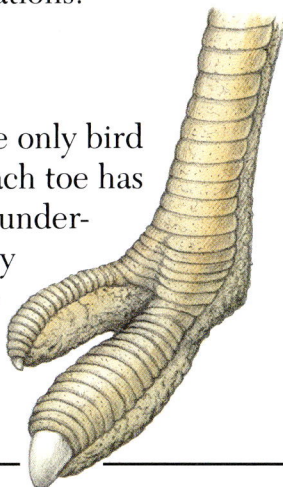

Egg sit

The male rhea makes eggs with as many as 12 different females. The females all lay their green or yellow eggs in the same nest, where the male sits on the lot himself.

The hummingbird

This is the smallest bird of all. You could hold one in the palm of your hand. It eats tiny insects and sucks nectar from flowers like a bee.

A hummingbird can flap its wings 80 times a second.

A hummingbird's feathers are iridescent, which means they change colour in the light.

Feeding and flapping

Hummingbirds hover while they feed, flapping so fast that all you can normally see is a blur of wings. They use up so much energy that they have to keep feeding to give them the energy to keep flapping.

Sipping through a straw

A hummingbird's tongue is like a long thin tube that sticks out from the end of its beak. With this special tongue, it can suck up nectar as if it had a straw in its mouth.

Soft and cosy

The hummingbird builds its nest from thistledown, lichen, and spiders' webs

Teeny tiny eggs

The world's smallest bird also lays the world's smallest eggs. It always lays two, each one the size of your little fingernail.

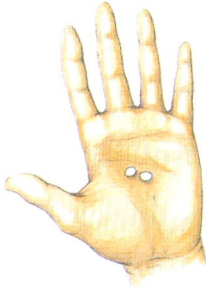

Flying champion

Three cheers for the hummingbird! It's the only bird in the world that can fly sideways and backwards.

Hummmmm

The hummingbird gets its name from the whirring sound its wings make.

Weak feet

Hummingbirds can't really walk. They have weak little feet that are perfect for perching but hopeless for hiking.

Glittering feathers

There are over 300 different kinds of hummingbird, and all of them have brilliant blue, green, or purple feathers. Some kinds have incredibly long beaks for reaching deep into flowers.

How birds fly

Birds fly in three ways: they glide, flap, or hover. Different birds use different kinds of flight. It all depends on where they live and how they feed.

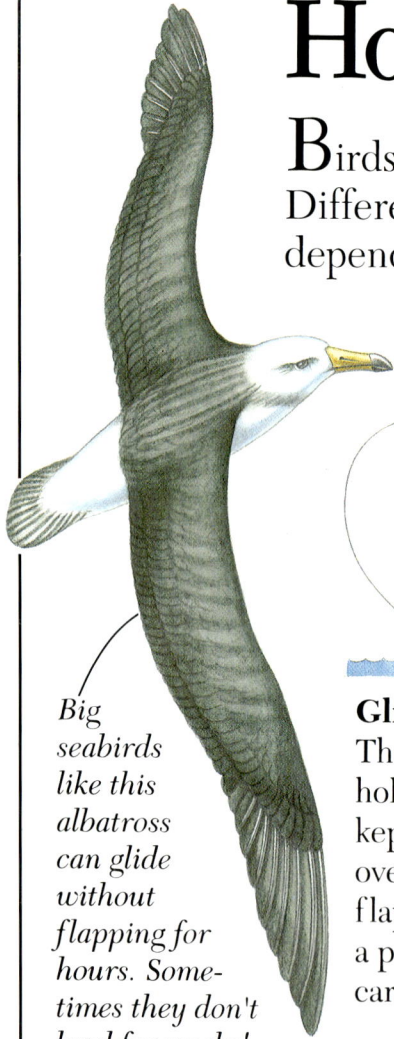

Big seabirds like this albatross can glide without flapping for hours. Sometimes they don't land for weeks!

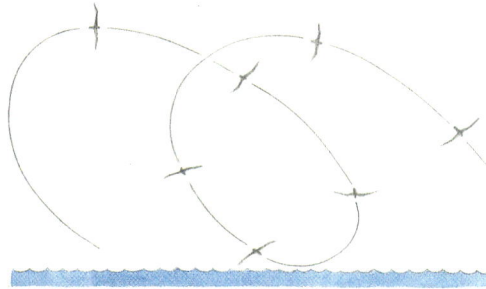

Gliding
This looks easy! When birds glide they hold their wings out stiffly and are kept up by the air rushing under and over their wings. But they have to flap every now and then – or find a puff of wind to lift them up or carry them forward.

Flapping
All birds flap. Flapping helps the bird to take off or climb higher in the air.

First the bird pushes down with its wings to lift it up and carry it forward.

Then it draws its wings up again, ready for another push down.

Hovering

Most birds cannot hover for long. It means flapping the wings so fast that the bird stays up in the air without moving – it just hangs there! Hummingbirds, terns, and kestrels are the best hoverers.

Kestrel

This bird is a kestrel, a sort of falcon. It is a very skilful flier that swoops down on mice and birds and carries them off in its talons.

Index